TEMPER

PITT POETRY SERIES

ED OCHESTER, EDITOR

TEMPER

Beth Bachmann

UNIVERSITY OF PITTSBURGH PRESS

Published by the University of Pittsburgh Press, Pittsburgh, Pa. 15260
Manufactured in the United States of America
Printed on acid-free paper
10 9 8 7 6 5 4 3 2 1
ISBN 13: 978-0-8229-6040-9
ISBN 10: 0-8229-6040-0

This book is the winner of the 2008 Donald Hall Prize in Poetry, awarded
by the Association of Writers and Writing Programs. AWP, a national
organization serving more than three hundred colleges and universities,
has its headquarters at George Mason University, Mail Stop 1E3, Fairfax, VA
22030.

for my sister, J. B. 1975–1993

...the imperfect is so hot in us...

—WALLACE STEVENS

CONTENTS

TEMPER

TEMPER

Some things are damned to erupt like wildfire,

windblown, like wild lupine, like wings, one after

another leaving the stone-hole in the greenhouse glass.

Peak bloom, a brood of blue before firebrand.

And though it is late in the season, the bathers, also,

obey. One after another, they breathe in and butterfly

the surface: *mimic white, harvester, spot-celled sister,*

fed by the spring, the water beneath is cold.

PATERNOSTER

The word for a line with a series of hooks also means the recitation of a
    prayer,
but in our case, a paternoster is shaped by the weight it holds at its end.

The leader and the link are determined by the shyness of the bite.
Reeling it toward you piques the bait.

Move closer. I want to tell you a story. It has its blood knots, its changing
    water,
the usual lures: family, violence, a margin left bare for interpretive remark.

It's not easy, even with this sinker, to go below the surface.
To ask you to offer me your open throat.

I'll start with the thing dragged up: the body of my sister.
I'll give you the location: the tracks.

The red treble designed to mock blood, to stick into the skin: one suspect—

our father—

Put this begging in your mouth, a decade of loaded beads.

First Mystery of My Sister

He unleashed the dog and waited, plastic bag in hand.
Sparky barked, nosed along the tracks

into the no-man's-property between station, line, and road.
Commuters numbed against the windows watched the nodding thistle

shiver as the 6:42 lunged toward the city. Overgrowth, long fingers
of grass, the bud of a dull tattoo—what remains—

her tagged body,
the dog at dawn sniffing a greening rose.

After the Telling

The conversation turns to paper
tapering at the edge

of the wall, the details of the interior.
You've put your hand

through my body and are caught
in the rack of vines

I've descended into.

You want to know what was left
for weeks in the weeds:

the trauma to the head,
the naked waist, my sister.

You ask whether the violence was domestic
and I tell you that an animal

nudged the bones, that afterwards,
someone put the dog to sleep.

I offer this as resolution. We turn again
to the space,

the crown molding, the framed faces.

Last Call

Come get me. A father in his nightshirt, a daughter on the end of the line
calling for a pickup.

A father in his nightshirt, in his stick shift, switches gears; the pickup
pulls up to the train station.

His stick shift switches gears. She's not there; he pulls up to the train
     station
bar, the cigarette machine, payphone.

She's not there; he drops change at the bar, the cigarette machine,
     payphone.
In the freight yard, a body

drops. Change crosses over a face in the freight yard. A body's
last words

cross over a face: a daughter at the end of the line calling last words,
come get me.

Quotes from the Papers

My mother's making the stranger
   —dirty, disheveled

in our doorway—a sandwich, turkey
   on white, quartered,

when he says:
   There's a lot of places to hide a body.

He lingers at the entrance,
   beneath the three kings

holiday card tacked at the keystone.
   The star, the angel

says, look to the east: *Check the train yard.*

God pointed his finger and said *step out of this body*: the guy who makes his bed from a ream of the free papers and squats at the depot, the janitor in charge of public toilets, the drunk Noah, an anonymous *ignudo*, my father. They stand against a row of black lines that resemble the nails knocked into trees to measure rising water, the reference points we use to gauge damage. They are numbered, but the numbers do not climb or descend; they offer themselves as *sin*: the endpoint of an arc. It's simple to picture these faces underwater because they boast no voice and exist only as outline, as a body traced in chalk. Because you've borne witness, you are asked to identify the man sketched from this description.

First Mystery of My Father

Yes, my father wanted to become a priest,
then met my mother, the story goes. I say

this because it is my nature to deceive you,
to pull on colors experience deems poison,

to keep you from tasting my skin. He left
seminary for the army years before they met,

which puts him in Germany transcribing
cipher, tuning his ear to the radio traffic.

It is here that I lose him, long before
I am born.

       Think of Eve. She saw
her father naked and felt ashamed.

Defense Language

The guard demands two skills in a signals intelligence analyst:
>interest in recovering clues that help answer questions,
>ability to remain alert while performing repetitive tasks.

It is 1966 on Devil's Mountain, Berlin. My father listens to whispers
over the wire, the key words for coordinates, arms.

He's been ordered to interpret, not translate, the voice he intercepts.
He knows the history of this cryptography: a sympathetic stain
between the lines of letters home—

Dear inamorato,
>The old man is ill.
A black petticoat confirms a message is ready.
I have given him a basket of oranges.
When you see me, do not betray your fever.

SECOND MYSTERY OF MY FATHER

This is the big one: the book that weighs on my father's lap.

He's wrapped in a blanket, flannel, scarf. It's December inside our house.
Behind the walls, the hot water in the pipes clots.

This is his Sunday ritual: highlighting the passages about redemption.

The pages are yellow; words rise as though spoken, boiled.

SORROWFUL MYSTERY

Something ancient burrows its white heart into the girl
left for dead along the side of the road, stoned past

the point of reflex. The opossum's tongue grazes her lip,
brushes the soft hair on her neck. You'd think it might

show a little sympathy for a thing so like itself: oblivious
to the breaching of bone, unable now to see anything

other than what must be an opening. It's light,
though, back home, it'll be hours before anyone stirs.

SETTING

A lilac can hold on, half-dead, for days
if it is not cut at dusk, when the dogs are wild
with its breath—

            still in the water, parted,

but a transit station is not a vase, despite the insistence
on light, despite the drainage gate or the tearing
of a pleated skirt,

            the perimeter laced

with ribbon, despite the spray cans, the cheap fever,
the dogs huffing, silver plated, no matter how much
I desire it cornered

            in glass.

PLOT

The man zips, stands up, no longer an animal
down on all fours, panting.
                        He's got a knot of bills

in his pocket, a bit of blood in his stubble, tacky
as lipstick.
                    He does not look down at the debris

browning along the edge of the switchyard wildflowers.

The head is damaged and cannot read this image.

Second Mystery of My Sister

It's impossible to define force, but it's not hard to figure
the size of an arrow drawn in a diagram of the free body.

Blunt.   Entry.
These cannot be measured like the integrity of a wing.

If you think of a torso as a box, you can see
how someone might want to open it with his fingers.

Rapt

When a man takes a woman from behind, she cannot see him,
even though, in this instance, she is prey. Her field of vision
is designed to capture sudden movement, not the lumbering

of his body at her back. She tracks the objects closest to her face:
the burlap grasses, the splayed legs of the railroad trestle.
If she looks at them with one eye and then the other, they shudder.

WOODPILE

Murder runs in our family tree.

Here is the portrait of our mother
out in the yard, in her housedress;

in her arms, she's holding split limbs
of paper birch (her father, his son,
                    my sister).

The black is an eye, the notch
a hatchet hollowed in the wood.

Behind her—the pyre, bonfire,
where pale strips of bark peel back and burn.

Talk Show

       My mother asks me to adjust the ears
    on the set. She dictates another letter to the host,
asking for airtime on the show for survivors, the one
with the telepath who channels

the dead and changes their substance
into the flesh beneath her bearded iris robe.
      Each season, she expands to hold the voices
         she's collected on her palate.

      I turn up the volume.
    The woman is crossing over like a broken helix
binding to another backbone. She's telling the audience
that on the other side

the physical is replaced
with frequency, that there is pattern,
      but that the peaks, when they fall,
        do not break.

Answering Machine

For some the telling is easy. The first confesses he's copied my number from the white pages, then claims the kill was not his first; his record is longer than the tape spooling the gears of this little box. He's already booked, sentenced to death, but wants a second hearing. It's common practice in the pen, a boasting of sums. The machine spits out this stenography. One leaves false leads: an earring, an accusation. The next, an anonymous tip: the tanker car, the foolishness of a girl to follow. My mother asks if they're calling me too, to ring her back. The last cracks a joke about crossing the road. I recognize this voice—it will tremble and plead forgiveness.

JOYOUS MYSTERY

It's not until the seventeenth century that ecstasy becomes rapture, *a*
    carrying off.
Prior to this, it is frenzy and displacement, void of the divine.

In the warehouses of the nineteen nineties, ecstasy reclaimed the early
    pleasure
of astonishment, an abandonment of the physical frame.

This morning the century shifts.

Envision this:
        your skin is warm, your movement evinces instinct,
        someone is touching you, asking if you've accepted your savior.

HEAVEN

Some would call this heaven—a teenage girl half-naked
in the grass. For all I know, they might be right.

The lighting is soft, midmorning, hazy enough to blur
the details, so we can fill them in any way we like.

Say, a brunette, barely legal, hidden.
From here, it looks like she's speechless.

//////////// ||

A New Way of Thinking About Space

In Giotto's cross we see for the first time
     the weight of the body
     pulling against the wood.

This is the moment after the accusation
     of the father, when
     the effects of gravity

take over. It's a break with the past,
     a refusal to stylize
     the holy, a rupturing

of the plane.

HELL

We call the division between the two parts
desire. They are near enough to spark.

Above the line, the woman is knocked out
like daylight beneath a door. Below it,

the men are agitated, aroused, estranged.
The dusk-loose gnats blood-speckle and splash.

HUNGER

In the open field, overgrown like a deadman's lawn,
mussed by young lovers,

a slackened corset drops.

A starved dog rubs his hide against a woman's leg.
From her thigh, she peels a strip of flesh and places it in her palm.

What she took for discarded clothing
                               rises up
                                       as a pack of animals.

I retell the story as myth, as if it were my own body devoured.

Nesting

Beneath the bridge, swallows mold the mask
of a woman's face,

clustering mud and tufts of hair dredged up
from a ditch,

leaving an interruption large enough to enter,
to spit wings,

which is an odd way to invoke annunciation,
a sudden blow.

The bones are narrow, so the birds take turns.
When it's over,

          the ground below whitens.

ERATO

Because of the struggle,
                 her arms and legs resisting,

you might take one look at the shape in the snow and say,

swan or *angel*,
               something to do with the divine, the light,

always, bending back.
                   Or you might remember the way

a girl's tongue razes ice or catches the root of the word

muse: an open mouth,
               a muzzle.

Signal Mirror

Given a settling of mercury,
grackles will walk onto a plank of water, scavenging,

bending over the folds of a blue dress without lifting it,
excepting the neckline, when they take flight.

You could say I'm revolving around another body.
Wind and other than wind, nothing.

Colorization

Black and white distances the viewer.

A broken crow drops from the jaw of some animal into the snow.
If we were to encounter it, with our chins tucked to our chests to block the
    blizzard,
we might think of it as shadow, but, in truth, the body is red.

There are two ways to define this: restoration and desecration.
It comes down to a question of actuality and intent.

When you enter my room, it is dark. What you can see
are broad patterns, the bars the blinds discard onto the linen.

If this were in color, would you know whether or not to be afraid?

Mystery Beneath a Handprint of Light

In another rendering, the repetition might add up
to something other than evidence.

A dog could signal devotion.
One sister: the object of desire.

With any luck, we would walk away
with a target, a seizure or a silver buckle.

When we look up here, we do not see Orion;
we see a silhouette shot full of holes.

PANIC

: the flushing of a flock after a trigger.

It's too early yet to assume the yellow heart of the hunter.

Water quickening in a drainpipe, the film on the moon—
light reflected from a surface startles.

Wind diminishes the shattering of wings.
If this were paradise, there'd be someone above watching.

Counting

When lightning enters the stitching of a woman's dress
and defiles it,

we do not avert our vision.
A material like this will not thicken when it's lashed

to loosen the dirt. It demands again illumination—
the quarter

of a second when a struck object appears to fall.

WEATHER

Rime constricts the limbs, composes the posture of receiving
crisis—the moment of turning

into force. The body is rigid, brittle as the bracts
pressed into a book, open

as a photograph of a girl on a glossy page;
the skin sticks as it thaws, blotting the fingerprints.

DECEPTION

There's no use in saying what if
it were warmer

and her skin doused with the sweat
of orchids:

the hammered back of an *Ophrys,*
Oncidium

cocked by the wind,
threatening.

Should it have happened then
(her body

written over in blossom),
the ripened bees

would have been faced with pollen—
honeyed, unhinged.

Mystery of the Noise the Air Makes When Milled

It's enough to force you over the edge
           and into the water.
This is one consequence of mining the sky
           to generate light:

murder, the rate of which rises in towns
           where the white blades
turn, driven by heat. Still, on a calm day,
           something is always

moving, suggesting a harness.

Mimicry

The wind kindles a pinwheel marking a roadside grave,
as if the spot
         where the body dropped held weight.

You could take this paper and cut it at the corners
to make a turbine or I could do it for you—
                        lick up

a pattern of green moths, bites in the sweet gum,
a husk of lace threshed
                in the attack, belonging

to someone young enough to sting of lit oil.

Answer to the Mystery of My Blank Stare

Since the skin around the eye is as delicate,
the first blow darkens to the size and shade

of the wings of a mourning cloak.
This is the problem with the living.

Someone says *look*
                        and you're supposed to say

it's beautiful. Instead, the tremor on the rock
is three days old. Later,

someone will point up at the moon.

Luminous Mystery

Darwin describes the death of God as the coming of light.
This happens slowly: a scaffold of singed paper

before it blackens; copper beneath corrosion;
the acoustics of the finch's song after a tear

in its vocal tract. Forget what you've been told.
Love is not immutable.

See this handful of birds I release on the church steps?
I do this to remind you.

GENE MAPPING

Imagine recovering a box of letters addressed to your father.
At first, the language is lost, written in the code of old lovers:
nicknames, allusion, errors in the script.

The woman, with her closed ovals and counterstrokes,
has something to hide. She will not offer the details
of initial encounter—small talk, skirted vision,

hemlines—but if you read her movement, bookmark
the pattern, you'll trace the message for the placement
of the hands, the blueprint for blue eyes.

TRACKING

Blood from a head wound thickens on the fingers
as if it's been reduced from bone.

Ask yourself, first, does he know he's being followed?

The print of his foot is not bound or reversed,
but he's bearing something heavy:

a hundred pounds over a shoulder
can collapse grass against the direction of the wind,

disturb a swarm of blowflies, or displace the water
burdening a leaf—the way a stray might when it turns

toward a sound before it continues feeding.

Sirens

Almost nothing can be destroyed by a voice. No matter how beautiful,
it's no weapon. Don't believe me?
Watch my mouth form the words
                              knife-hand or *hammer-fist*.

Still standing? Now come here. I want to teach you this trick
my father picked up
                    a blow to the back of the ear—hit and stick.

The sirens scatter. One of us is too wrecked to rush.

Supple

When the word *supple* parts my lips, some men snicker
but I'm not thinking of a certain skin or of brained leather,

but of how the weak gain dominance through leverage,
turning a woman onto her stomach until she tries to rise.

When pressured, the bones also respond.

Spit

Usually a face is destroyed gradually
by something typical—age or light—

tanned by the same motion my father
applies to shine the shoes of the men

at the club; squatting on the locker room
floor he scoured clean that morning

with bristles and a salve the scent of lime,
the muscles in his arm clench, wearing away

the imperfections.
                Now and again, a face is
rubbed out by the back of a blackened hand.

CONCEALMENT

Darkness cannot disguise the form of the human body,
the skull in relief: the inion, the helmet shell.

Any man in my family will tell you that
the head needs to be cut up with camouflage—

scrub stripped from the perimeter with a uniform grip—
that a shirt should never be torn off in the open.

Exposed skin glints like a bull's-eye, which is why
we pattern it with charcoal, burnt cork, lampblack or bark.

EVASION

The ice fixed on a river that does not bend
is limber.
            Without an artful approach to measure

warmth—white fog, white ribs protruding as though
the surface
            were wanting—without an arc,

the weight of a body is best stretched parallel
to the low
            profile of a man worming across a set

of tracks.

Betrayal

If I stand dead center between two men and aim
a finger at each,

> my body is square with the ground.

If one man steps backward, the second appears closer
although he has not moved.

> If I turn toward him,

I can no longer follow the path of the other man
slipping behind the hill.

> This leaves you and me staring

over each other's shoulders each time we embrace.
When we are this close,

> I cannot look you straight

in the eye. I can only draw myself up, against your mouth.

Radio

Always assume someone is listening between lifts in the silence
to discover your location and destroy it with fire.

This has little to do with a painted face on flayed skin:
over a radio, a voice travels in all directions.

*Report that you have seen signs of certain things, not that those things
actually exist.*

Glorious Mystery

Even Christ mourned the glory before the world was,
the grief we feel in dropping out of heaven. In the alley

below my apartment, two kids addicted to glass
cannot stop moving. One climbs the wall

between the dumpster and the escape.
The other clubs her fist into her thigh, sparking

her cigarette. They're no angels but they're trying
to get back to the knowledge of the first time.

Finishing Moves

We begin by leaning, learning the feel of the other body
before extending it into its longest possible line

but finishing is different from this partnering:
it is more like a property let go, where a female crawls

to birth a litter, the ground teeming with weeds, choked.

Mystery Ending with a Girl in a Field

You've heard it before—but listen:

> *I brought you into this world,*
> *I can take you out of it.*

I know what you're thinking.

Maybe he did. Maybe he didn't.
Nothing's resolved. But what does it matter?

I could snap these petals off all day,
mouthing *he loves me, he loves me not.*

Cold Logic

We love a thing we cannot know.

This is what stops us from touching
but also what cannot stop us from touching

a body even after it's cold.
Some call it continuous, this mystery—

I keep coming back to the grass that grows
near dumpsters, that startles my leg after dusk.

In the black bag is the fruit I bought and did not eat,
so soft against the knife it wasn't worth saving,

the way it did not part to speak or run.

Elegy

No shepherds. No nymphs. Maybe just one:

the girl the fawn strips like a fisherman's rose.

Death turns its mouth red. It can no longer lie

in the lilies. Not on my watch. The lake is filthy

with silver fish sticky with leeches. Lovesick,

I flick a feather into the water. No stones.

Only the one in my pocket, heavy as a tongue.

NOTES

The epigraph is from Wallace Stevens's poem "The Poems of Our Climate."

"Hell" is a description of Duchamp's *The Bride Stripped Bare by Her Bachelors, Even (The Large Glass)*.

The phrase "a sudden blow" in "Nesting" is the opening of Yeats's "Leda and the Swan."

The last line of "Radio" is a direct quote from the U.S. Army field manual *Combat Skills of the Soldier, Appendix E Tracking*; the "painted face on flayed skin" is Michelangelo's, from *The Last Judgment*.

ACKNOWLEDGMENTS

I wish to thank the editors of the journals where these poems first appeared:

AGNI Online ("Mystery Ending with a Girl in a Field," "Mystery of the Noise the Air Makes When Milled"); *American Poetry Review* ("Defense Language," "Elegy," "Erato," "First Mystery of My Father," "Heaven," "Paternoster," "Second Mystery of My Father"); *Antioch Review* ("Hunger"); *Blackbird* ("Colorization"); *Black Warrior Review* ("After the Telling," "Answering Machine," "Answer to the Mystery of My Blank Stare," "Betrayal," "Cold Logic," "Counting," "Deception," "Evasion," "Finishing Moves," "Glorious Mystery," "Hell," "Mimicry," "Mystery Beneath a Handprint of Light," "Nesting," "Panic," "Rapt," "Setting," "Sorrowful Mystery," "Weather"); *Gulf Coast* ("Joyous Mystery," "Luminous Mystery"); *Kenyon Review* ("Gene Mapping"); *LUNA* ("Concealment," "Radio," "Sirens," "Suppleness," "Tracking"); *Ploughshares* ("Temper"); *Prairie Schooner* ("A New Way of Thinking About Space," "First Mystery of My Sister," "Last Call," "Quotes from the Papers"); *Southern Review* ("Spit," "Talk Show," "Woodpile"); *Tin House* ("Second Mystery of My Sister").

"Colorization" was reprinted in Heather Sellers's *The Practice of Creative Writing: A Guide for Students* (Bedford/St. Martin's, 2007).

"Nesting" also appeared in *Best New Poets 2007*, edited by Natasha Trethewey (University of Virginia Press, 2007).

"Colorization" (2005) and "Setting" (2007) were reprinted by *Verse Daily* (www.versedaily.com).

Many, many thanks to Karen Fish, Andrew Hudgins, John Irwin, Greg
Williamson, Stephanie Bolster, Alan Shapiro, Mark Strand, Michael
Collier, Catherine Barnett, Bret Lott, Mark Doty, Mark Jarman,
Lorraine López, Kate Daniels, Rick Hilles, Nancy Reisman, Paul
Young, Liz Hazen, Alex Long, James Hoch, and Alex Lemon.

Warm thanks also go to the Bread Loaf and Sewanee Writers'
Conferences and to the Tennessee Arts Commission for scholarships
and grants that allowed me to complete the book, and to everyone at
AWP and Pitt.

I am forever grateful to Lynn Emanuel for selecting the book.

And to Brian, for picking me up.

Made in the USA
Monee, IL
09 October 2022

15522590R00049